Women Warriors

Unveiling the Strength of Women of God

NEGIEL BIGPOND

PERFECT CIRCLE
PUBLISHING

Tulsa, Oklahoma

Unless otherwise indicated, all Scripture quotations are taken from the
King James Version of the Bible.

Scripture quotations marked NASB are taken from the *New American
Standard Bible*®. Copyright © 1960, 1962, 1963, 1968, 1971, 1972, 1973,
1975, 1977, 1995 by The Lockman Foundation. Used by permission.
(www.Lockman.org).

19   10 9 8 7 6 5 4 3

Women Warriors: Unveiling the Strength of Women of God
ISBN 13: 978-0-9667234-4-1
ISBN 10: 0-9667234-4-9
Copyright © 2009 by Negiel Bigpond
P. O. Box 97
Bixby, OK 74008

Published by Perfect Circle Publishing, Inc.
10026-A South Mingo Road #440
Tulsa, OK 74133
www.perfectcirclepublishing.com

DEDICATION

This is dedicated to my mother, Lilly Bigpond Sims, who raised me to pursue the gifts and callings of God on my life and to honor the gifts and callings of women.

TABLE OF CONTENTS

FOREWORD

For the past decades God has raised up a new generation of Native American leaders with tremendous insight into the things of God. Many of these leaders, such as Negiel Bigpond, have the ability to write and speak about the power of God manifested through their cultures. We need the revelation written in these pages to be complete in the body of Christ today.

Among Native peoples, this book is destined to raise the dignity and understanding of the valuable role of their women. They have fought in the spirit for their people through atrocities that we, at least in the white community, are just barely beginning to grasp. As Dr. Bigpond so aptly reveals to us, the women have been the backbone and strength to the Native people and to him as a person.

Native women know how to war. If I have to go into a spiritual battle, I want warriors like them fighting alongside me and watching out for my back. Many are the most prophetic people I know because of the seer ability God has given to the host peoples of the land.

All men and women around the world need to read this book because it will change who you are and make you a better mother, father, brother, sister, and friend. There is a sense of gratitude modeled by a Native patriarch and Christian leader that sets an example for us and for generations to come.

I am always humbled when I am around my friend Negiel Bigpond because of the wells of wisdom in him. He has overcome great obstacles in his life but has the ability to bring great joy and laughter into the gloomiest of situations. He learned that the joy of the Lord was his strength from previous generations of Native people. And he is not afraid to seek counsel from women intercessors today—regardless of their color or cultural background. This makes him a secure man and a great model for the next generation of young warriors.

There are deep waters running through this book. It has the ability to flow right through your soul and make changes in you that forge even greater intimacy in your relationship with Jesus Christ. The words of this book are strong and weighty, yet refreshing and humble. Open the pages of this book and be blessed by its rich fruit. Take a drink of its wisdom and you will be forever changed.

Cindy Jacobs

Generals International

Dallas, Texas

March 25, 2009

Therefore I, the prisoner of the Lord, implore you to walk in a manner worthy of the calling with which you have been called, with all humility and gentleness, with patience, showing tolerance for one another in love, being diligent to preserve the unity of the Spirit in the bond of peace.

There is one body and one Spirit, just as also you were called in one hope of your calling; one Lord, one faith, one baptism, one God and Father of all who is over all and through all and in all.

But to each one of us grace was given according to the measure of Christ's gift.

Therefore it says,
"When He ascended on high,
He led captive a host of captives,
And He gave gifts to men."

Ephesians 4:1-8 NASB

9

PREFACE

The idea of *Women Warriors* came to me as I was studying and seeking information about our tribal culture in the Euchee Nation. I began to see how our Native women played a big part in our military battles. There were women who fought right alongside the men in war, and they were great "gifts to men."

Today in our modern American army, we are just catching on to this idea that women are good fighters. They have a strong sense of patriotism and a passion for justice that is equal to any man's. Overall, it is true that men are physically stronger than women. But we also know there are some women who are as physically strong or stronger than some men.

When I saw there was an historical precedent for women being in battles in the natural realm, I really wasn't that surprised. For years I had prayed and ministered alongside women and had been awed by their effectiveness in spiritual battles. When I was a boy my mother's prayers were not something I wanted to cross! Since I have been married, have had two daughters, and now have granddaughters, I see how important and powerful it is when a woman agrees with me in prayer or ministers alongside me.

In 1997 Jay Swallow of the Cheyenne Nation and I formed the Native America Circle of Prayer, now called the Native America Apostolic Prayer Circle. Its purpose was to pray for Two Rivers Native American Training Center and all Native issues, on and off the reservations. Native people and tribal leaders from all over North America began calling us to pray for them, and this continues to this day. When other non-Native ministries began hearing the praise reports and victories, they also began calling for prayer support.

Through the years a few men have been a part of our group of prayer warriors, but—as usually happens in most church prayer meetings—it has always been mostly women. My personal adventure with these great women of God is something that I will devote a chapter to, but for now I will just say that it has been both humbling and enlightening!

We men can learn a lot from the women in our lives who pray for us, stand with us, and minister with us. They spend so much of their valuable time calling out to God for our well-being and success, and they serve in so many vital ways in our families and churches. I encourage husbands, fathers, sons, grandfathers, nephews, uncles—and all my brothers in the Lord—to turn to the women God has put in your lives and pray with them. Ask them to stand with you in faith. Receive their gifts and their callings. You will discover what I have discovered: There is great power and tremendous victory when you ride into battle with *Women Warriors.*

CHAPTER I

Mom: Spiritual Eyes

The first woman warrior I knew was my mother. She taught me about praying over the land. She would go out and walk over it, pick up the dirt, bless it, and talk to God as she walked. She felt the wind, watched the eagles soar in the sky, and gave thanks to God for all of His creation. She showed me that our Native people had the great privilege and honor of praying over the land God had given us. We were to bring His presence wherever we went on the land.

Mom fought in faith right alongside my father, who was the third generation of Methodist ministers in our family. Women in those times were not allowed to do a lot in the Methodist Church. Only the men prayed out loud during the services. The women didn't feel slighted or dishonored, though. This was just the way things were done then. And believe me, my mother made up for it at home! She did a lot of praying out loud in both English and Euchee around our house.

The congregation of my father's church was mostly poor people, and there were lots of people who came and stayed with us from time to time. It was understood that we would just take care of them. Mom fed them and took care of them while they were with us. She could make a feast for many out of so little, and I'm convinced Jesus was there multiplying fry bread and meat again and again. I never heard her complain or get angry that we didn't have enough. And she was the fastest cook I have ever seen! It seemed to me she could cook anything at a moment's notice.

Women warriors are great givers, and so was Mom. She always gave whatever she could give to help people. She was always helping someone. It meant a lot to me that when I went into the ministry she gave twenty dollars or more every month into our ministry until she died. That was a lot for her.

Although the women didn't speak in the church services, Mom was a Bible teacher. She taught Sunday school to the kids, and I remember her reading her Bible every day. She was always giving away those little pocket Bibles to people. Truth was one of her standards, and not just biblical truth. She was very blunt and to the point. She never sugarcoated anything!

There was a lot of racism against Indians at that time, and I became aware of this when Mom worked at a Laundromat for a while. I remember her saying the customers were mean to her, but we had to forgive them and go on. We weren't to make a big issue of it. She was not just teaching me how to pray and get my needs met; she was teaching me how to walk in the character of God in tough situations.

Women warriors are tremendously hard workers, and Mom was no exception. As you can imagine she was always busy doing something, with four kids, not much money, and people coming in all the time to feed and take care of. She was a great combination of Mary and Martha. She knew how to sit at Jesus' feet while making a meal and tending to us kids. She had those special times alone with the Lord, walking the land and praying or reading and studying her Bible, but the rest of the time she was working to make everyone else's life better.

Mom was also a peacemaker. She could get as mean as anybody, but when everyone got into a big dispute she was the one who would try to keep the peace in the family. Now that I am older, I understand the strength and patience it takes to try to help people calm down and see things from another person's point of view. And it takes a lot of perseverance to get people to look at the bright side of all their problems.

THE CONVICTING POWER OF A PRAYING MOTHER

Now I have painted a pretty perfect picture of my mother, but she could also be a force to be reckoned with. It was my mother who gave most of the whippings, although both my parents were really strict. Most of the time I was respectful and pretty obedient to them when I was at home, but I did not always live the way they would have liked me to live when I was away from the house, especially in my teenage years.

As I got older I began to notice even more that although the whippings had made a great impression on me, Mom's prayers were even more powerful. I remember I came in after a night of messing up and flopped down on our couch. I fell asleep there, and when I woke up Mom was standing over me. I just knew she was going to get all over me. I prepared myself for the worst when she said, "How are you, Son?"

"All right, I guess." I was shocked she was so calm.

"Glad you made it home all right. I was praying for you."

I knew that she knew I was messing up. I also knew that one of the reasons my foolishness had not gotten me into serious trouble was because she had been up praying for me. This did more to convict me of my wrongdoing than harsh, condemning words. In fact, it was probably worse! Her love and prayers were much more convicting than if she had given me a long, angry sermon.

MIXTURE OF FAITH AND TRADITION

In those days we seldom went to medical clinics or doctors, and it seemed that if anything came along I got it. Whether it was measles, chicken pox, the flu, or something else, I caught it from the other kids. My mom and dad always prayed and relied on God to heal us. They would pray until the fever broke or the crisis passed. I'm here today because of their faith-filled prayers in a loving Father who heals. But there was also a strong Native influence mixed in with their Christian faith.

Mom was the "doctor" of the family, and she would often take us to a medicine man or a medicine woman for what today people would call a "natural" cure with herbs and such. These medicine men and women were Christians. They believed in Jesus, but they also practiced many of the old

16

Native ways and traditions when it came to medicine. They were more like natural doctors, but they were also very spiritual. With Native people, everything is spiritual.

Even though the people I grew up with were Christians, superstition was the basis for some of the things that were done, especially when someone died. For example, I was eight or nine when my uncle died, and after seeing him in the casket at the funeral I kept seeing him other places. When I opened a closet door or walked into a room, there he would be, standing there. I told Mom about this, and she scolded me for not taking the "medicine" after the funeral.

After a funeral there would be a pot of liquid containing roots and herbs that the medicine man or medicine woman had prayed over. You would wash with it and drink it to let the departed go. This was supposed to keep you from seeing them again or having bad dreams about them. If you saw them, it meant you had not let them go by taking the medicine and you were calling them back.

When my uncle died I did not drink the medicine after the funeral, and so afterward I began seeing him. Mom took me to the medicine man, who gave me something to wash with and drink. Then he prayed over me, and I never saw my uncle again. Of course, after I began really reading and studying the Bible, I saw it was not God's will that we should see our dead relatives everywhere we go! Today we just release our dead into His hands and go on doing what He's called us to do. That old tradition of drinking and washing helped us release our loved ones in the past, but it is not something we practice anymore. Now the Word is our medicine.

Over the years I have had to repent of some of the things I believed and practiced growing up because they were old Native ways that did not line up with God's Word. But the one thing all Native people have that some other cultures lack is a deep spirituality. Everything is seen with spiritual eyes. We trace all that happens to us first in the spirit realm. This is how all true warriors are too.

THE POWER OF STORIES

Jesus knew the power of a good story. He knew that a good story inspired warriors to live right and fight the good fight of faith. In our family, Mom was the main storyteller. Sad stories. Scary stories. Funny stories. There was the one about an elderly Native couple who were on their way to the Methodist campmeeting. They were looking for the campground and got themselves lost. Finally they came to the edge of the town and saw all these cars and trucks out in a field. Many of the hoods were up, and all of them looked old and beat up. They knew this must be the place. They pulled in and soon realized it was a junkyard! This was just one of the many stories Mom told that taught us to laugh at our difficulties.

Mom was a warrior who knew how to laugh at every device of the enemy. Through the years and since she has been gone, laughter has seen my family and my congregation through many struggles. Even in the most intense battles, I learned from Mom that a good story or a funny comment could make all the difference. The Bible says that God sits in the heavens and laughs at the enemy, so we should too.

Then there were the scary stories. One of the ways Mom got us to obey was by telling us scary stories, usually as the sun was going down and just before going to bed. This was something the old ones did to keep their children quiet at night. She would tell us that if we moved around a lot we would draw the evil spirits. This made us kids very serious about going to bed and going right to sleep.

We were also told that it was best to play during the day. Run through the woods when it was light. But as soon as the sun started to go down, you best get home because there were all kinds of evil spirits in the woods at night. Native people always seem to see lights going through the woods. They see this as evil spirits carrying lanterns. It was made clear to us kids that the safest place for us to be at night was sitting quietly at home or asleep in our beds! That way the evil spirits wouldn't bother us.

This is another example of a traditional Indian way that we do not practice anymore. As Christians we learned we are people of faith not fear, and we raise our children in faith. We don't make them afraid of evil spirits. We teach them their authority over them in Jesus Christ and tell them stories and testimonies to build up their faith in God. Our children go to sleep in peace.

Mom told us lots of stories at night that reinforced our spiritual view on life and death. One of my favorites was the story of when my grandfather, her father, passed away. This involves another one of those old Native ways regarding death.

When someone died, it was tradition to saddle a horse and tie it up outside the church when the casket was brought in. The horse was what the dead person would use to ride off into eternity. Then for three days we would have services and eat together. On the last evening we just ate very bland food—nothing fried, salted, or sweetened—and left food locked up in the church overnight. This was to honor the spirits of our Christian ancestors who were coming to get the one who had just died and lead them into Heaven.

When my grandfather died, the horse was tied and the services were held. The last night after the service the bland food was left, the church doors shut, and the horse left tied out front for the night. Then, as the sun began to rise the following morning, the horse started whinnying and bucking. People nearby heard this noise and ran out to see what was happening. That horse was acting like someone was trying to get on him!

There was one story that was both funny and scary. It was traditional in those days to put miniature houses over the graves. These were big enough for a man to crawl into, and the purpose was to put the deceased's possessions in it because it was their new house. One day it was raining, and one of our elders was walking by the graveyard (normally

Indian people don't hang around graveyards). This was a white elder who didn't know about the traditions, and he got into one of these houses on a grave to get out of the rain. When one of our Indian elders passed by driving his horse and wagon, the white elder flew out of the grave house, waving his arms to get a ride. He never got a chance to ask because the Indian took one look at him, whipped his horse, and was gone in a flash!

Mom's stories are still very strong in my memory, but today I don't follow many of her old Native ways. I do follow her way of telling stories about Jesus, though. I tell my children and grandchildren about all the great things He has done and still does for us. He came to give our souls rest. He is the Prince of Peace. And we are to have sweet sleep in faith not fear.

I have to say, though, even with all these scary stories, I always knew Mom's prayers and faith in the Lord had the last word in our home. And her stories served to give us kids a spiritual view on everything in life. That was part of a great legacy she gave us.

THE HARDEST BATTLE

Looking back as an adult, and now that I have a family of my own, probably the hardest thing my mom and dad went through was when my little brother passed away. He was just a baby when he got sick. I was pretty young, about five years old, and I remember my mom carrying him, nursing him, and then seeing him in a little casket. I remember that both my parents were so sad. He was named after my father, so that made it especially hard.

As a pastor I have seen Christians turn from the Lord in bitterness and anger when He didn't heal their loved one like they prayed and expected Him to. I have seen parents go into long periods of depression, and it seems like when their child died they died. I look at my own kids and know it would be a terrible heartache if any one of them went home to be with the Lord before I did, but then I remember my mother.

I think the greatest test of a warrior, whether man or woman, girl or boy, is dealing with the casualties of war. We have an enemy who hates us because we love Jesus. The devil will take any opportunity to steal from us, kill us, and destroy us. Our Father is much greater than he is, and the weapons of our warfare are powerful, but every now and then the serpent will slip into our lives and bite us. This is when we can either give up or grow into greater faith and glory.

I thank God my parents chose to be comforted by the Holy Spirit and grow stronger in the Lord when my baby brother went to Heaven. Maybe they were comforted by the fact that he got healed in Jesus' arms instead of being healed in their arms. But one thing they knew for certain. They would see him again in Heaven one day.

Now that I have children and grandchildren of my own, I have so much more respect for Mom. The greatest battle is seeing a child go home to Heaven before you do, and she managed to pull through that terrible battle in faith, trusting Jesus even more.

A MOTHER'S PRAYERS

There are no more fervent prayers than a mother's prayers for her children. That's why the devil attacks mothers and makes them feel like they are too emotional about their kids to pray for them. But God is emotional about His kids too! It is a godly thing to be passionate when we pray for our children.

I've seen women who scream at the sight of a spider become a force to be reckoned with when that same spider came near their children. The enemy knows this and wants to convince these women that demons or sickness or rebellion are different than that little old spider. He tells them they are not strong enough spiritually to pray and believe God for their own children. But I know from years of watching my own mother, my wife, and now my daughters: If you are a mother, you are a woman warrior!

When their children are in trouble or any child they know is in trouble, a woman can go to war in prayer like no other. It always amazes me how many women come to me to pray for their kids because they just don't believe their prayers are powerful. I tell them the truth. The devil is lying to them! They are the best ones to pray for their children. Somehow my mother knew this. She never doubted God's Word was true, that He loved her, and that He loved her children—even after my brother died.

Mom was a great woman warrior because she loved Jesus so much, she trusted Him and His Word, and she loved His people. She worked hard and she prayed hard, and I still feel her prayers today. I'm still learning from her today. She gave me a spiritual foundation and view of life that I am passing on to my children and everyone around me. So in that sense, her faith and prayers are touching lives she never met.

Mom opened my spiritual eyes and showed me how women warriors' lives and prayers continue to impact the generations that follow them.

CHAPTER 2

Jan: A True Friend and Lover

The Bible says that when a man finds a wife he finds a good thing, and he obtains the favor of the Lord (Proverbs 18:22). I know some husbands might disagree with that, but I am not one of them. One of the best decisions I ever made was to marry Jan. Any success and joy I have today could not have come without her in my life. She is a lot quieter than most women, but she is a great warrior.

When I talk about women warriors, most people immediately have a mental image of a prophetess declaring a word from the Lord or an intercessor passionately crying out to God. But after years of participating in spiritual warfare, I'm convinced that the greatest women warriors are those who love and stand by their husbands and leaders in the church no matter what happens or how they are treated.

Few women are recognized for quiet endurance in the faith, but they are the backbone of the church. These are the ones who, when a crisis or calamity happens, bring calm and wisdom. They are in the background, operating in gifts of hospitality, thinking of the little details that make people's lives easier and better. By example they show the rest of us how to persevere and seldom waiver in hope and faith when times are tough.

Jan has always been very involved in the church because she oversees the finances and she knows people in the community. She was born and raised here, and she went to all the traditional Euchee ceremonies, which is our tribe. When I met her in high school in the tenth grade, I had come out of boarding school, so I didn't know many people in the community or in our tribe. Through the years I have learned a lot from her and relied on her as we reached out to the community with God's love.

Jan has a lot of favor with the Creek Nation because she has worked for them for years. She is a great liaison with them to obtain grants and funds for various needs of the church and the school. In all these ways, she contributes to the ministry and makes my life and the lives of our congregation so much better.

Through the years I have watched Jan take food to families whose relatives had passed away, oversee wedding and baby showers, honor the fathers on Father's Day, care for the children in the nursery when no one else volunteered, take a turn cleaning the church every month (and sometimes twice a month), oversee the finances of the ministry, and help me keep the extensive grounds of the church and Two Rivers looking nice. I'm sure no woman has spent as many hours on a tractor mower as Jan!

Other than being my wife, though, the most important ministry to Jan is taking care of our children and now our grandchildren. The reason I have been able to go out and minister is because I know everything is okay at home. I never have worried about my family while I was away because Jan was there. She is the reason I am able to minister as I do. I am truly living what God promised in Proverbs 18:22. Being married to Jan is not only a good thing, but also she brings the favor of the Lord to my life.

FAITH AND ENDURANCE

Jan and I were just out of high school when we got married, and back then I wasn't the holy, sanctified man of God I am today! She put up with a lot from me before I really surrendered my life to the Lord and began to pursue a godly life. (She still puts up with a lot, but now we are serving the Lord together.) I always knew I was called to the ministry, but it wasn't until after we started having kids that I got serious about it.

When I began traveling in the ministry, going to reservations and other churches, our children were very small, so most of the time I would go alone. It was tough for Jan to be home alone with little kids, but she endured it. I believe raising children and being at home with them is one of the greatest tests of a woman warrior. It is the highest calling of a woman, because God made them to give birth and nurture.

We would take the children with us when they weren't in school. We traveled to many reservations, preaching the Gospel and praying for people. Obviously, there wasn't a lot of money on the reservations, and we couldn't live off the offerings, so I always had another job or odd jobs I would do.

There were times when we had no money, and Jan would work with me to make ends meet. We had our disagreements and misunderstandings like any other couple, but I never felt she was not supportive of me pursuing what God had called me to do. She has sacrificed a lot to stand with me in the ministry, and she has had to have great faith and patience during trying times.

I remember one ministry trip Jan and I took together, without the children, to the reservation at Pine Ridge, South Dakota. The church where we ministered took up an offering, but it wasn't enough to get us home. We left the reservation with $25 in our pockets! On the way home we stopped at a prophet's house. He blessed us with a meal and gave us some money to fill up the gas tank, so we thought we'd be all right.

We were following another evangelist who said he knew a shorter way home, so he was leading the way. Unfortunately, he got lost and we went the wrong direction for a while. We soon parted company with the other evangelist. Jan and I just kept praying and believing God would multiply the gas we had, and every time we came to the top of a hill, I would coast down to save fuel.

Jan always packed a cooler with food and drinks to save money on meals. So we enjoyed our bologna sandwich and water, which was all that was left. By the time we got to Kansas both of us were exhausted, so we pulled over to sleep for about twenty minutes or so. Three hours later we woke up! Off we went again, and by the time we started into Tulsa we were on empty and penniless.

In Tulsa, near the intersection of Highway 75 and 71st Street, there was a big hill. Going up the hill I gunned the engine to get some momentum for going down the hill. A policeman saw this and pulled me over. I explained to him what I was doing, but he wrote me a ticket anyway. We pulled into our driveway on fumes, and we were $50 in the red because of the ticket. Times like that you need a wife who understands and stands.

One time Jan and I and the kids went to the Crow Reservation in Montana. We traveled in an old, brown Dodge van that was as ugly as sin. By this time the kids were old enough that they were embarrassed to be seen in it around town, but they loved to travel long distance in it because it was roomy and comfortable inside.

We were driving through Billings, which had always been known as a racist city, on a four-lane highway. These two white guys drove up beside me, made an obscene gesture, hollered at me, and then passed me. I got mad, started yelling at them, and went after them. I drove alongside them and yelled at them to pull over because I wanted to get out and "teach them a lesson."

Jan told me to stop and think before I did something that would cause more trouble than it was worth. I let the other car go on and pulled over to the side of the road. I was still really angry but she continued to talk quietly to me, and her words were calming me down. Finally I came to my senses. I turned around and apologized to the kids for my actions. I told them that what I had done was not God's way. Then we all prayed together.

Warriors are not afraid to confront something that is wrong, and they know the right way to do it. Jan didn't start screaming at me, condemn me, or disrespect me in front of the kids. She understood why I was angry, and she was probably angry about what had happened herself. But warriors know how to deal with their anger. She threw it at God, just talked quietly to me, and imparted some good, common sense. She proved she was a courageous and disciplined warrior that day. I shudder to think what might have happened if she hadn't been with me!

A TRUE SERVANT

As the ministry grew, I began to be asked to travel and to be a part of conferences and meetings around the country while Jan was always in the background. There was one trip that seemed like it was a complete waste of time in the beginning, but in the end it turned out to be a miracle breakthrough we had been praying about for a long time.

First, I'll give you some background. In 1992 I felt called to start Morning Star Evangelistic Center, which is now Morning Star Church of All Nations. We met in an old trailer that had been at my brother's house. It had been hit by

lightning, so he let us have it. Jan and I and our congregation fixed it up and moved it to the land behind our house.

After about a year the Creek Nation gave us a smaller
trailer. We made it into a kitchen for the church, so we would
have a place to eat and fellowship together. Later we got
another trailer for the children's ministry. Finally the
Methodist Women gave us a double-wide trailer that we still
have today. It became our main church building and was also
where Two Rivers Native American Training Center classes
started. But we knew that we needed a permanent church
structure, and we began to pray and believe God for it.

In 1996, in faith, the men in our church poured the foundation for a new building. It sat for two years, but we kept
praying and believing. Then in 1998 Jay Swallow and I were
invited by Ed Silvoso to attend a big conference in Dallas.
There was a great revival going on in Argentina, and some
evangelists from there were coming to talk to church leaders
in America.

When we got to the meeting, we set up our little table
telling people about Two Rivers, but few people were interested. There were a series of events that made us feel some-
what slighted, and we really weren't sure why we were there
after awhile. Then it happened. Ed Silvoso began speaking
and asked Jay and me to come up.

Ed told the American church leaders that some of the
biggest mission fields in the world were the Indian reservations in America. He told how Jay and I had spent decades
traveling to these places where no one else would go because

there was no money in it. The only thing you are going to reap on the reservation is souls! He also told them about Two Rivers Native American Training Center and our vision to multiply ourselves, to train up the next generation to win souls and establish churches on the reservations.

Then Ed took up an offering. We were touched as leader after leader came up and put checks and money in the offering baskets, but we were astounded when we counted it all up. It was over $150,000—enough to finish the building that would house Two Rivers and our church!

That was one of the most exciting reports I had for Jan. We built the building soon after that, and Cindy Jacobs was our keynote speaker at its dedication. It was a glorious time of celebration in which we looked to the future in our new church and school home. The double-wide trailer that was our old church and school is now the Two Rivers Library, and the other three trailers have been disposed of, as they were in pretty bad shape.

Something else significant happened because Ed Silvoso brought us and the vision of Two Rivers to the attention of so many church leaders. Suddenly Jay and I were asked to speak at major meetings across the nation and overseas. It seemed wherever there was an Indian needed, Jay and I were invited.

Jan expressed some concern that I was becoming "the token Indian," and there were times when I wondered about it. Her counsel caused me to be more prayerful about where I went. There was no doubt God was putting Jay and me in a visible place where we could bring Native issues to the attention of the church all over the world; but I had to keep my eyes on what God was doing, avoid getting carried away with all the attention, and accept the invitations He wanted me to accept. Then I didn't worry about why people were doing what they were doing because I knew what God was doing.

After that meeting in Dallas, Jay and I were in great demand in another way. As the church grew in the understanding of the restoration of the apostle to the body of Christ, major church leaders recognized us as apostles. Then pastors on the reservations and off the reservations began coming to me, saying, "God has told me that you are the apostolic leader over my ministry and church. If that bears witness with you, would you please be my spiritual father? Would you teach me, challenge me, and hold me accountable?" My ministry was expanding in ways I had never imagined.

During all this excitement and traveling Jan was usually at home. Although our children were grown, she was working full time to make ends meet. Our congregation was very small, and it could not afford my salary. My traveling and ministering were expanding to churches that would give me an offering, but I was still going to a lot of places that couldn't. Jan stayed home to work and do whatever she could at the church. She had to stand in the background while I was put in the limelight. Everyone was talking about me, and no one was mentioning her.

Through all the tough times and the challenging situations, and while I get all the attention and travel all around the world, Jan remains the same. She never has been jealous or envious of me. She has always remained supportive and worked hard to help bring the vision God has given us to pass. She is a servant who inspires everyone around her, including me, to be a servant; and this is one of the greatest character traits of a true woman warrior.

MATURITY AND TRUST

Earlier I said that when people think of women warriors, they usually picture a prophetess or intercessor. I didn't mean to imply that Jan was not prophetic or that she never interceded. My wife's prayers are powerful, and God will give her a word for people from time to time because she really cares about them. Many people's lives have been touched and healed and set free through her prayers—including mine!

There are times when Jan will minister to the people with me. And sometimes when I'm away, she will give the message or lead the services. Although it is not something she feels called to do, she is a great minister when she does it because she is a giver, and she has so much wisdom and experience to share.

Great women warriors are not selfish and self-centered. They don't try to promote themselves. They look at the big picture and play their part in God's plan. That is what Jan does, and that is one reason why she is a great warrior for the Lord. Since I am on the road so much, and most of the time Jan stays home, I am grateful that she is as mature as she is and that our marriage is based on trust in God. We have to trust Him to lead us as individuals, especially when we are apart.

For example, when Jay and I formed Native America Circle of Prayer, most of the prayer warriors were women. We would go on these prayer journeys, and there were times when a group of five or six of us would climb into the Morning Star van and go to places within the state of Oklahoma or across the country, sometimes staying in hotels overnight. It was usually Jay and me and a bunch of women, but there have also been times when I was the only man in the group.

I'd like to say that all these women through the years were holy and never looked at me with lust in their eyes, but that is not the case. There have been a few that I have had to keep at arm's length until they got the message, and some God just moved out because they refused to get the message.

There have also been times when one of these women would come up to Jan and me, ignore her, and start talking to me about situations and meetings that Jan knew little about. Some wives would resent all this and get really insecure, but Jan never has. She's secure in her role as my wife and in the church, and she knows she can ask me if she wants to know what they are talking about. That's maturity and trust.

We also have had to learn how to communicate as a couple while I'm on the road, and I have had to become more aware of her feelings and concerns. I call her often but she never expects me to call. Someone asked her once, "Does he call you every day?" She said, "No, why should he?" But I do call and check in to see how everyone at home is doing and if she needs anything. This is for my security and safety as much as hers.

My wife is a warrior, but she is still a woman! In my early years of ministry I had to learn to come to grips with the fact that I needed to prove my love for her so that she could remain at peace while I was away. We both had to grow up in this. She had to learn to trust me and I had to prove I was trustworthy. I had to see over time that she could and would handle things at home and remain faithful to me.

A lot of Christian ministers get divorced because a minister becomes successful and noticed and the spouse feels slighted. We didn't really know we were avoiding this by working out our problems through the years, but now I can look back and thank God I have a wife who stayed and worked things out instead of leaving—another character trait of a great woman warrior.

I'm glad Jan enjoys who she is and what she is called to do, despite all the challenges and crises she has to deal with. She doesn't really care about going on a lot of these trips with me, but we do well together when she does. When we launched Two Rivers I was at home a lot more, but the demands of the school were great. Now we have to raise money to keep the buildings maintained and to see the rest of the vision fulfilled, and she is my greatest helper!

One thing she has always done is to steward the land with me. I get on the big John Deere tractor and she gets on the little riding lawn mower and we cut the grass every week when it's growing. Some couples play golf or go to the lake, but Jan and I cut the grass! Through the years she has been a great sport about things like this. It was the way things were, and she flowed with it.

True women warriors keep their eyes on what's important and don't get sidetracked by the everyday attacks of the enemy—or having to cut grass! They deal with all the difficulties and challenges, but they don't lose sight of the big picture. That's Jan. She knows there is a vision to fulfill. It takes maturity and trust in God to remain strong and focused, and I can look back over the years and see how my wife has developed these things in her life.

AN ABLE MINISTER

The new building and more attention from national leaders were great, and the demands of ministry increased as a result. Now I have more pastors and emerging leaders looking to me for counsel and encouragement. It is wonderful when Jan can come with me to the reservation churches I oversee. She is a good listener and has a lot of wisdom. She's not the kind of woman that will bust out speaking just because no one else is. She will seek God and wait for Him to give her direction. Then she will speak directly from her heart.

Jan has always sung with me, and now the whole family is involved in our music ministry. No matter where I am, I can ask her to join me on the platform, and she follows me and blends in with all the musicians and singers. She understands the power of the anointing in worship and flows with the Holy Spirit.

Through the years people in the church, especially women, have tried to get Jan to lead the women's group or teach a Bible study, but she does not believe that is her calling. I have a great respect for her because she has not compromised her calling. She has not let congregation members pressure her into doing things she knows she is not called to do. When I ask her to teach one of our services she does a great job, but it isn't something she feels called to do all the time.

A great warrior always sticks to what God has called them to do and does it with all their heart, soul, mind, and strength. That describes my wife! She is my best friend and lover and the greatest gift God has ever given me besides Jesus.

CHAPTER 3

Mary Fish: Understanding Authority

Through the years I've known some great women of God who have taught me, but the first—and probably the greatest influence on me in growing up as a minister—was Mary Fish. Through the years she truly has been my spiritual mother, as she has been to many others. She taught me about authority, and I'm not talking about having authority over the enemy. I'm talking about learning to submit to the authority of God and those He has called you to serve.

Learning to submit to authority is sometimes easier for women because most cultures teach their women to submit to their husbands. Little girls grow up looking for their knight in shining armor, who will come and make their lives perfect. They search for someone they can look up to, which naturally turns into submission. But most women figure out pretty quick that no man is their perfect knight in shining armor! Then they might have a struggle with submission too.

Being a strong-willed man who was out to prove himself, God sent Mama Fish into my life. She was an anointed, Pentecostal Osage woman who really scared this young Methodist when I first saw her. She was short, had her hair up in a bun on the top of her head, wore a black, long dress, and preached fire and brimstone. She invited the Christian band I was playing in to come and minister at her Greyhorse Reservation. I had heard about these wild Pentecostal people; but she liked us even though we played Christian rock music, so I respected her and liked her even while I was afraid of her.

Mama Fish was a minister who traveled to different churches and campmeetings on the reservations, and sometimes she would bring us along to do the music. I was in my thirties and full of myself, but she loved me and saw the call of God on my life. When my band split up, she asked me to continue to travel with her and lead worship from my keyboard. She taught me how to play the old Pentecostal way on the piano, and she led me in the baptism of the Holy Spirit. She also began to teach me, correct me, and sometimes rebuke me concerning the Word and ways of God. Being with her was like being in my own personal school of ministry—and she could be tough!

At one campmeeting I was feeling my oats. She told me to get up and sing a song, but I got up and started testifying and preaching. She gave me a few minutes of disobedience and then marched right up onto the platform beside me. I turned to her and stopped speaking. With the fire of God in her eyes she said, "What'd I tell you to do? Did I tell you to preach?"

"No Ma'am."

"Did I tell you to read the Bible?"

"No Ma'am."

"Did I tell you to testify?"

"No Ma'am."

"What are you supposed to be doing up here?"

"Leading worship, Ma'am."

"Then I suggest you start doing that."

Never did a young man get to his keyboard so fast!

I was embarrassed, but I'm glad I received her rebuke. If I had gotten offended and gone off in a huff, I never would have learned to respect and follow the instructions of my elders in the church. I never would have learned to honor the authority God had given them in my life and trust Him that I would be blessed and grow up in God if I obeyed their instructions. God was training me to follow His orders. He was using Mama Fish to show me what it meant to be a man of God who understood the Holy Ghost power and favor that come from submitting to authority.

THE WOMAN ISSUE

Lots of denominations would have had a problem with Mama Fish rebuking me in a church service. In fact, they wouldn't have allowed her to preach or teach or have any kind of leadership role in their church. Some denominations believe that women should be silent in church, mainly because of the following passages of Scripture:

Let your women keep silence in the churches: for it is not permitted unto them to speak; but they are commanded to be under obedience, as also saith the law.

And if they will learn any thing, let them ask their husbands at home: for it is a shame for women to speak in the church.

1 Corinthians 14:34-35

Let the woman learn in silence with all subjection.

But I suffer not a woman to teach, nor to usurp authority over the man, but to be in silence.

For Adam was first formed, then Eve.

And Adam was not deceived, but the woman being deceived was in the transgression.

1 Timothy 2:11-14

There are five reasons I believe the teaching that women should not speak or minister at all in a church service is wrong, and they all relate to a lack of understanding of what the Bible is really saying.

1. **Paul was not talking about preaching and teaching or giving a word of the Lord.** The word used for "speak" in 1 Corinthians 14:34-35 is not the Greek word that means "logical, reasoned speech," like a preacher or teacher would use. The Greek word translated "speak" literally means jabbering and going on about nothing, like a child who is just talking

nonsense.[1] So I don't believe Paul is saying a woman cannot speak in a leadership capacity in church. I believe he is just telling women to stop disrupting the services by whispering and carrying on when they are supposed to be listening.

2. **Paul was dealing with the culture of his time.** In Paul's time the Jewish women who got saved knew to be quiet and listen in church because they had never been allowed to say anything or participate at all in their synagogue or the Temple. But the Gentile women who were being saved in places like Corinth and Ephesus had no idea how to behave during a church meeting. They were disrupting what the Holy Spirit was doing by foolish talking, and Paul had to address it. Paul never meant they should not speak or minister at all. He just wanted them to do it decently and in order (1 Corinthians 14:40).

3. **The Bible gives many examples of women being active in leadership roles.** Although the tradition in the Jewish synagogue during Jesus' time was that women were not allowed to speak and could take no active part in the service, remember who was in charge during that time: the legalistic Pharisees and Sadducees! Throughout the Old Testament there

---

[1] See Spiros Zodhiates, *The Complete Word Study Dictionary: New Testament*, (Chattanooga, TN: AMG Publishers, 1992), #2980.

were great women in leadership, judges like Deborah in Judges 4:4 and prophetesses like Miriam in Exodus 15:20.

In Joel 2:28 Joel prophesied there would come a time when "your sons and daughters shall prophesy." In Luke 2:36 the Bible tells about Anna, the prophetess who prayed in the Temple and lived to see the baby Jesus. Later, under the New Covenant, women became even more active in ministry. Philip's daughters prophesied to Paul in Acts 21:8-9, and one of the greatest examples was Priscilla, who taught Apollos with her husband Aquila.

And a certain Jew named Apollos, born at Alexandria, an eloquent man, and mighty in the scriptures, came to Ephesus.

This man was instructed in the way of the Lord; and being fervent in the spirit, he spake and taught diligently the things of the Lord, knowing only the baptism of John.

And he began to speak boldly in the synagogue: whom when Aquila and Priscilla had heard, they took him unto them, and expounded unto him the way of God more perfectly.

Acts 18:24-26

Priscilla also traveled and ministered with her husband Aquila and Paul. (See Acts 18:18, Romans 16:3, and 1 Corinthians 16:19.)

4. **The context is husbands and wives not men and women believers.** I believe 1 Corinthians 14:34-35 and 1 Timothy 2:11-14 talk about the women as wives, especially in 1 Timothy 2:11-14. Paul is saying (my paraphrase), "Wives, don't go jabbering on and on about nothing to your husbands in church. Stop asking all kinds of questions while the service is going on. Wait until you get home. Then talk about these things with your husband. And don't be disrespecting and trying to dominate your husband by thinking you know more than he does and you need to teach him what you know. Remember, Adam was created first and he was the head of the home."

"But I suffer not a woman to teach, nor to usurp authority over the man, but to be in silence" is not talking about just any woman and any man in the local church. It is talking about a husband and a wife. The Greek word translated "man" also means husband,[2] and Paul goes on to talk about the relationship between Adam and Eve. So in context, we should take this to mean husband only.

5. **Jesus always had strong, faithful women around Him.** Mary, His mother; Mary Magdalene; Mary and Martha of Bethany, who were the sisters of Lazarus; the Samaritan woman, who preached the Gospel to her town and got them all saved; the woman with the

---

[2] James Strong, *Exhaustive Concordance of the Bible*, "Greek Dictionary of the New Testament" (Nashville, TN: Thomas Nelson Publishers, 1984), #435.

issue of blood who risked her life to touch Jesus' robe and receive her healing—all of these women were powerful women warriors. When Jesus was crucified, most of the men who followed Him fled, but the women stayed with Him through everything.

I think it is a shame that so many churches keep women from ministering. They are missing so much! They have no idea how rich their spiritual lives could become by allowing the women to flow in their gifts and to do what God has called them to do right alongside them. I thank God that Mama Fish knew better and had the courage to demonstrate this scriptural truth in my life.

PROPER RELEASE AND SUPPORT

Mama Fish showed me how a woman of God can be a wife, mother, and minister in the right order. She ministered with the blessing of her husband and was under the authority and counsel of a group of elders in their church. She knew she had a call of God on her life to minister, and she took that seriously; but she also took the call of God to be a wife and mother seriously.

God created male and female and made a powerful statement: It is not good for man to be alone. We always apply this to the function of marriage. We think that a man must have a woman to cook, clean, keep the home running right, give birth to the children, and then train the children. But God was talking about everything in life when He said that it was not a good thing for man to be alone; and He commissioned both Adam and Eve to have dominion, keep, guard, and be fruitful and multiply in the Garden.

When Jesus came, He sent His disciples out two by two. The Bible does not say that some of these disciples were women, but it also doesn't say that they were not women. It simply doesn't say. He sent seventy out, and most likely there were women with their husbands, like Aquila and Priscilla, as well as women with other women, like Mary and Martha, who went out to preach the Gospel and develop the disciples.

Just as Jesus released and supported these women and the apostle Paul released and supported Aquila and Priscilla, I believe that a church authority must release and support women warriors today. Support is more than a word of encouragement now and then. Support involves relationship, accountability, and vision.

If the woman warrior is married, she should go out with her husband or be released by him to go with a suitable partner in ministry. A husband and wife are one, and they are equal partners in the kingdom; but the husband is the head of the wife (Ephesians 5:23). A woman warrior respects this and knows the value and safety of it.

Some women do not seek or wait for proper release by their husbands or their leaders, which leads to many problems in the body of Christ. Women who rebel against their husbands and aren't accountable to any apostolic or pastoral authority can cause a lot of trouble. Instead of honoring their husbands and spiritual leaders, having faith in God to move on their behalf, using their gifts wherever they can, and continuing to grow in God while they wait for the proper release, they just go out and start ministering. Great things may occur in their ministry, but their marriages and families suffer. They also suffer because they don't have the right support. In the end, their lives don't give a good witness for the Lord.

It isn't always all the women's fault, though. Some husbands and church leaders are too afraid or proud to release and support women in their gifts and ministries. These husbands and church leaders should realize that when they hold back these women from ministering and refuse to allow them to move in their gifts and callings in their churches—they are opposing God. A husband who opposes his wife ministering or a leader in the church who is against women using their gifts and fulfilling their callings is going against God's will.

Now I am also aware of the issues of timing and maturity. As a leader, sometimes I realize that a woman is not ready to be released. The Bible says in 1 Timothy 3:6 that it is dangerous to put a novice, or someone who is not mature enough, into a position of authority in the church. When I release a woman to preach or teach or to be the head of a particular ministry, I want to do it when the Lord tells me she is ready. Otherwise, I put her in danger and I put the rest of the congregation in danger. (I have learned this the hard way with both men and women!) This is why it is important for women warriors to be submitted to, held accountable by, and released by an apostolic or pastoral authority. It keeps them safe because they will be more likely to have their inner lives as well as their outer lives in order.

Having the right covering and support are particularly important for single women and wives whose husbands are not saved or are opposed to their ministry, but all women warriors need to be submitted to a leader in their church. This helps to avoid the appearance of evil, keeps all their relationships right, and maintains their good witness to their friends and family. This was something Mama Fish showed me.

UNDERSTANDING A WOMAN'S PASSION

Traveling with Mama Fish, I saw how women warriors are sensitive and can get emotional. That's why they need support from men. Women are powerful in the kingdom and in battle because they understand the process of giving life to this world. A woman has the ability to carry life, nurture life, and love life. She gives protection to life in the womb, and then the man helps to carry, nurture, and protect that life after it is born. There are the inside battles and the outside battles in any war; there is the battle to see the baby born and the battle to raise that baby to maturity. Just as husbands and wives join together to fight the natural battles of life, Christian men and women join together in apostolic, biblical order to establish God's kingdom in the Earth.

Unfortunately, some women simply refuse to take the instruction and correction of their leaders. Instead of submitting to the authority God put them under and bringing their carnal emotions and thinking in line, they become offended and leave church after church angry, hurt, and even bitter. When these women come to me because they have heard I have a heart for women being released into their ministries, I have been able to help some. It just depends on whether they are willing to change or not. They must forgive, be healed, and submit to me as their spiritual authority for me to properly release and support them.

It is also unfortunate when women warriors are misunderstood and set aside by men in leadership. There are a lot of truly wounded women warriors because pastors and leaders did not see they were a gift from God and develop them, or in some cases these women were so gifted and anointed that they intimidated the men in the church. Many of these women are not in fellowship in a church as a result. We need them and must encourage them to take their place in the local church, forgive and be healed of their past wounds, and to continue to grow up in God and their gifts and callings.

From Mama Fish, I learned that a woman warrior is teachable and strives to control her emotions. She will persevere in prayer in order to speak and act according to God's Word and the direction of the Holy Spirit instead of her own personal feelings or agenda. Because she is fully submitted to and respects the authority of her husband and her apostle or pastor, she can get the emotional support and balance she needs from them. She takes their counsel and guidance seriously.

Overall, a successful woman warrior's emotions are submitted fully to the Word and the Spirit, as well as to her church authorities, so that the godly passion she brings to the battle is pure, is welcomed by all warriors, and is pointed in the right direction.

MAMA FISH'S COMMISSION

As I traveled and ministered with her around the country, Mama didn't just tell me to be courageous about the truth; she lived it right in front of me. God had commissioned her to walk in Pentecost, and that wasn't easy, especially as a woman. Many church people on and off the reservations turned on her, and the enemy used ignorant believers to persecute her for believing what the Bible said about speaking in tongues and moving in the gifts of the Spirit.

Then I caused her some more trouble. Some of the church people didn't approve of Christian rock music. They thought it was of the devil, but God showed Mama that all things were originally created by God. Satan just perverts them for his purposes, and the Church has given away a lot of blessings because we assumed that something was from the devil when its original creation and purpose were from God.

Mama also saw that a new generation was expressing their worship of Jesus in this music. She knew we were the future. She took us all on in spite of all the criticism, and then later when our group disbanded, she took me on to train and teach. That really got the tongues to wagging—and I'm not talking about the gift of the Holy Ghost! They didn't think it was right for her to teach a man. Nevertheless, she just kept on doing what the Bible and the Holy Spirit told her was right. She taught me as Priscilla taught Apollos.

I watched Mama go through some really difficult times, and this is what I saw. She was not alone! She was not only submitted fully to the Lord and what He had commissioned her to do; she was also fully submitted to her husband and the group of elders who oversaw her life and ministry. She was teachable and listened to them and the Holy Spirit. She was not a lone ranger out there trying to make a name for herself on her own. She knew that was the way warriors got killed. So she surrounded herself with good men and women of God who would give her wise counsel and back her up in prayer.

It became obvious to me that Mama's success in ministry, even in moving in the power of God when preaching and praying for people, was directly related to how she was connected and submitted to God and the other authorities He had put in her life. When it came to me, Mama would not let go until she saw me walking in the same way. She showed me and taught me that ministry was more than just fancy preaching, great music, and miracle power. If I had no regard for authority, if I was not right with God and in divine order in the body of Christ, my ministry was not going to go very far and my prayers would become hollow words.

THE GREATEST LESSON

As I submitted to Mama's authority and did what she told me to do in faith, something great happened. I began to hear the voice of the Holy Spirit more clearly and obey Him more quickly. That's what happens when you fall into line as a warrior. When you come into divine order in the church, you come into more wisdom, more discernment, and eventually more responsibility. And you get more powerful because you are not out there alone. You have all kinds of other great warriors fighting alongside you.

I found out that obeying my elders was a major key to my success in God, both as a person and as a minister. The more obedient I became, both to Mama and to the Holy Spirit, the more both she and the Holy Spirit could trust me. When God and the elders know you can be trusted, you will find yourself being entrusted with more and more vision and authority yourself.

Now don't get me wrong; when I was working with Mama, she wasn't always perfect. I also saw her weaknesses and problems, but that didn't stop me from receiving from her. I knew God had placed her in my life to teach me and train me, so I didn't allow myself to get critical or offended, even when she corrected me in public. I repented of my sins, forgave any offense, and concentrated on all the good things she was imparting into my life and ministry.

The Bible says that promotion comes from the Lord, and in God's army warriors are promoted as they prove themselves in obeying orders and being faithful where God places them. I will always cherish my time with Mama Fish, and I thank God He brought her into my life at that crucial time. I don't believe my ministry would be as rich and effective as it is today if I hadn't submitted to her as unto the Lord. By both word and deed this great woman warrior gave me a powerful understanding of authority.

Chapter 4

The Circle: The Power of Prayer

The formation of Two Rivers Native American Training Center by Jay Swallow and me birthed Native America Circle of Prayer, now called Native America Apostolic Prayer Circle, but we have always referred to it as "The Circle." We started this prayer group in the trailer that is now the library, which is also where we first held Two Rivers classes and Morning Star services. I had grown up around my mother, who was a praying woman, and had been taught by Mary Fish, but the women God brought into The Circle were all kinds of women such as I had never experienced!

Through the years these women have been all colors and cultures and backgrounds, but they have had one thing in common: a deep love for the Lord and a total hatred of the enemy. Most of these women have been prophetic, and a few of them actually stood in the office of the prophet. We have always had our share of unusual experiences, and we still make corrections along the way; but overall we have seen again and again how our prayers support Native ministries and stop the devil in his tracks.

The Circle began in 1997, when Jay and I realized that we needed steady prayer support for all we were doing on the reservations and through Two Rivers. In the beginning there were just three women, and they would sit together and ask God what He wanted them to pray about. Sometimes they would pray over the land that Morning Star and Two Rivers was on. Sometimes they would pray over our prayer requests. And other times they would take off to different parts of our city or our state they believed the Holy Spirit was leading them to pray over.

The leader of The Circle in the beginning was an able minister and fellow Euchee by the name of Betty Pulver. Betty and her husband Al had been in ministry together and have been associated with my ministry for many years now, but Betty knew she wasn't called to lead The Circle. So she and the other two women began to ask God to bring in more prayer warriors, as well as His leader for the group.

In 1998 The Circle began holding weekly prayer meetings on Wednesday mornings, which we still do today. I was present more and more to give my prayer requests and find out what God was telling them about the direction of the church, the school, and my ministry. The discussions got to where everyone was talking at once or they all had a word from the Lord, so I brought out the old Native talking stick. Native people would sit in a circle and the chief or the one in charge would hold the talking stick. If he didn't give it to you, you couldn't speak. This was my way of bringing order to our meetings. We all had a good laugh about it, but it worked!

Praying people would come and go, mostly women, but a few were beginning to attend regularly because they knew

God had called them to pray with us. One of those women was a Cherokee woman named Ada Winn. The Holy Spirit had witnessed to Betty when Ada came in November of 1998 that Ada was the leader they had been praying for. She told Ada, "One day you will be the leader." Ada wasn't too sure about that, but she was open to whatever God had for her. One year later, on November 21, 1999, which was the second anniversary of The Circle, Ada became the leader, and she still is as I write this.

At one time The Circle had fifteen to twenty regular members, which is the most we have had so far. From time to time some of the members will travel with Jay and me to various conferences and meetings, supporting us in prayer and giving us prophetic direction and encouragement. Some of the members introduced us to other major leaders in the church, which increased our connections in the body of Christ. Again and again we have seen how the prayers of these women warriors made the difference in the power and effectiveness of our ministries.

The Circle has traveled throughout the state of Oklahoma and to reservations in other states to pray over the land. They also go to the reservations to teach about intercession, locate the prayer warriors there, and establish more prayer groups. Then they continue to be in contact with and support these groups. All of this is under our apostolic authority and support.

Over time, as Jay and I would travel and be with other leaders, these ministers began to call The Circle for prayer.

Many of them are Native Americans, but some are not. Although The Circle has been devoted exclusively to Native American issues and ministry, their prayers have supported all kinds and all colors of people from all over the world.

We have discovered that many people will trust an Indian because they know Indians understand pain, injustice, and the process of forgiveness that must happen to get free of these things. Indians also have a clear understanding that we have a spiritual enemy, and until you stop what the devil and his demons are doing, you are not going to get the victory in your life.

"TRAINED KILLERS"

Sometime during my years with The Circle, I began to affectionately refer to these women warriors as "trained killers." I saw that they would not stop until the enemy was defeated in their lives, in the lives of their loved ones, and in the life of anyone who asked them to pray for them. They despised the devil and everything he did to kill, steal, and destroy in people's lives. If anything even smelled evil to them, they were in the throne room talking to God about it, getting His Word on it, and then declaring what He said about it. They would not rest until that thing was settled for good.

Over the years I have identified twelve characteristics of trained killers. Every prayer warrior has them—no matter what age, gender, culture, or color they are. Their skill in spiritual warfare is based upon their godly character.

1. One who is able to endure the pain of a defeat in battle and get back up to win the war.

2. One who is able to listen.

3. One who is able to stay focused.

4. One who is able to recognize godly and ungodly authorities.

5. One who is able to move quickly with understanding, knowledge, and wisdom when they have to.

6. One who does not fear change.

7. One who is teachable and trainable.

8. One who seeks and finds what is needed.

9. One who understands covenant.

10. One who lives by grace, truth, mercy, and peace.

11. One who always goes forward and never looks back.

12. One who knows how to give and receive honor in God.

I based this list of characteristics on many passages of Scripture. One of them is 2 Corinthians 11:23-28:

> **Are they ministers of Christ? (I speak as a fool) I am more; in labours more abundant, in stripes above measure, in prisons more frequent, in deaths oft.**
>
> **Of the Jews five times received I forty stripes save one.**
>
> **Thrice was I beaten with rods, once was I stoned, thrice I suffered shipwreck, a night and a day I have been in the deep;**

In journeyings often, in perils of waters, in perils of robbers, in perils by mine own countrymen, in perils by the heathen, in perils in the city, in perils in the wilderness, in perils in the sea, in perils among false brethren;

In weariness and painfulness, in watchings often, in hunger and thirst, in fastings often, in cold and nakedness.

Beside those things that are without, that which cometh upon me daily, the care of all the churches.

Paul was a prime example of one who carried the authority of God because he carried out God's purpose and plan no matter how hard it got. He was not afraid or embarrassed to be a fool for Christ. Although he cared about people, he didn't care what other people thought of him. He only cared what God thought of him and what God wanted him to do for Him and His people.

Paul cared so much about God's people that he went through every kind of battle a believer can go through to care for the churches God had given to him to oversee. He was a hard worker, persecuted and beaten, stoned, imprisoned, left for dead, shipwrecked, in peril everywhere he went, without food and drink at times, exposed to all kinds of weather— and in all that he had an intense sense of responsibility to the churches God had called him to plant and nurture in the faith. He wasn't just an apostle by title. He was a spiritual father to these people. This is the kind of compassion and dedication I see in The Circle.

Like Paul, the motivation of a "trained killer" in The Circle is a combination of their love for their Savior and Lord and their love for those who belong to their Savior and Lord. They war for the souls of people and hold nothing back. Like Paul, when they walk into a town the demons scatter, the world's authorities shake, and the Holy Spirit moves mightily to save, heal, deliver, and set free whoever believes in Jesus. I have seen this happen many times as I have traveled with members of The Circle. They mean business!

Another passage of Scripture where I found characteristics for trained killers is Jeremiah 1:4-12, which says:

> Then the word of the Lord came unto me, saying,
>
> Before I formed thee in the belly I knew thee; and before thou camest forth out of the womb I sanctified thee, and I ordained thee a prophet unto the nations.
>
> Then said I, Ah, Lord God! behold, I cannot speak: for I am a child.
>
> But the Lord said unto me, Say not, I am a child: for thou shalt go to all that I shall send thee, and whatsoever I command thee thou shalt speak.
>
> Be not afraid of their faces: for I am with thee to deliver thee, saith the Lord.
>
> Then the Lord put forth his hand, and touched my mouth. And the Lord said unto me, Behold, I have put my words in thy mouth.

See, I have this day set thee over the nations and over the kingdoms, to root out, and to pull down, and to destroy, and to throw down, to build, and to plant.

Moreover the word of the Lord came unto me, saying, Jeremiah, what seest thou? And I said, I see a rod of an almond tree.

Then said the Lord unto me, Thou hast well seen: for I will hasten my word to perform it.

Trained killers are called from the womb to war against evil and bring peace wherever they go—and they know it. They are sure of their calling, and they are powerful in prayer because they understand the power of God's Word. They stick to the task until it is finished, no matter how hard it gets, because they have God's Word on it.

Women warriors don't just tear down the evil and pull down the strongholds; they build and plant the Word of the Lord to bring forth a new harvest of souls, peace, and prosperity. They establish new circles of prayer and train intercessors to carry on. They are commissioned by God to pray for the release of His will in the Earth and in people's lives. And they do all this by keeping an intimate relationship with God and the spiritual authorities He has placed in their lives.

INTIMACY WITH THE FATHER

In Jeremiah 1:8 God tells Jeremiah not to be afraid because He is going to be with him. This is the foundation of a woman warrior's life: intimacy with the Father. All the women warriors I have respected and appreciated guard and protect their time on the mountain with God. They seek Him in special times of prayer, and then they seek Him and talk to Him all day and sometimes all night. They know that no one knows them and what they are going through like God does, and He holds all the answers. He has a strategic plan for the battle they are facing, and the more they know Him the more they will understand His plan.

This is like what our Native warriors would do before physical battles. Whenever a battle was about to take place, the warriors would go to a sacred place to be saturated in the presence and wisdom of God. They knew that their primary objective was to bring God's peace to the people of the land. The strength to war was used only to bring peace, so they had to have total peace with God before they went into battle.

All Christian warriors get their strength and ability to make war from God. They know what the Bible says, that God teaches us to make war. No one knew this better than David, who said, "Blessed be the Lord my strength, which teacheth my hands to war, and my fingers to fight" (Psalm 144:1).

Great warriors also know that you can't just go out on the battlefield swinging your sword and shouting loudly. You have to have God's battle plan and strategy. When women warriors get a word from the Lord in their prayer time, they have His plan, His strategy for victory; but they don't stop there or just run out and do it. They also find out how to handle the word from the Lord right.

Warriors know that when God speaks to us and deploys us or commissions us to a task, He whispers it to our hearts, and a seasoned prayer warrior will also hear from the Holy Spirit if they are to share their task with someone and who to share it with. Sometimes it is for them to pray through alone. At other times it may involve one or two others. And sometimes it can take a whole platoon of prayer warriors to pray and agree.

The military wording for this is strategic planning, and strategic planning also involves "stealth" or "covert" operations. Not every mission is to be known by the whole body of Christ or the world. Every mature woman warrior I have known walks in this wisdom, and it is what makes them so effective in prayer. They tell on a "need to know" basis, and the "need to know" is determined by Jesus, their Commander in Chief, as well as those He has put in authority over them. Knowing this is one of the keys to their success, and the only way they can walk in the knowledge of His will, His strategic plan, is to maintain that intimacy with the Father.

In Jeremiah 1:9 God placed His hand on Jeremiah's mouth and said that He was putting His words in Jeremiah's mouth. "Then the Lord put forth his hand, and touched my mouth. And the Lord said unto me, Behold, I have put my words in thy mouth." This is one of the most striking pictures of the Father being intimate with one of His chosen warriors. He did a powerful thing. He breathed His Word into Jeremiah when He commissioned him to be a prophet to Israel—and women warriors will not go out to battle until He breathes His Word into them.

POWERFUL MEDICINE

Our Native people will look at someone who is very spiritual and say they have "powerful medicine." Women warriors have "powerful medicine" because they are continuously seeking God's wisdom and ways. They pour over God's Word to know His mind on whatever they are praying about.

Believe me, when a woman warrior comes out of her prayer closet after a powerful encounter with the Lord, she manifests every characteristic of a trained killer! The enemy is scared to death at the very sight of her. *But she is not mean.* Her time on the mountain with the Lord brings great joy to her heart. I have seen women warriors giggle like schoolgirls and even have fits of laughter as they released the word of the Lord and beat the enemy to a pulp!

I used to think that laughing and giggling were just fun and released stress. But the Bible says in Proverbs 17:22 that "a merry heart doeth good like a medicine." Now I know that laughter and joy are the health and strength of a prayer warrior. I have always enjoyed a good joke, but laughing in the Spirit accomplishes amazing things in the human spirit. Joy and laughter enable us to release the power of God into the world and completely destroy the enemy.

The Bible says that God sits in the heavens and laughs at all the evil things the devil is trying to do (Psalm 2:4). It also says that our victory over the enemy happens when we can laugh at whatever he throws at us.

Behold, God will not cast away a perfect man, neither will he help the evil doers:

Till he fill thy mouth with laughing, and thy lips with rejoicing.

Job 8:20-21

I have seen women warriors express all kinds of emotions in The Circle, but the most amazing is their ability to laugh in the face of the enemy. They know he is no match for the Word of God and the Spirit of God. Laughter is powerful medicine!

PERSONAL MINISTRY FOR UNITY

I have talked about how the Native warrior would get ready for battle by going to a sacred place. Part of the process of preparing themselves to fight was to purge themselves of anything not pleasing to God. This included being healed of any old wound from the past. They knew that soldiers who had deep wounds from past battles would not be able to fight well and were likely to get killed.

The warrior would sit before the Creator and begin to release any anger or hurt, jealousy or envy, strife or contention, unforgiveness or bitterness—any kind of wound, whether it was spiritual, mental, physical, or emotional. They did not want to go into the next battle carrying wounds from the last battle. Mature women warriors know this.

There have been times when I would bring prayer requests and issues of concern to The Circle, and as we talked or began to pray it would become obvious that someone in the group needed personal ministry in a certain area of their lives. One thing I have learned from women warriors in The Circle is that the most powerful prayers are prayers of unity and agreement, and you cannot be in unity and agreement if one of your members is "out of joint" in the body.

We would stop everything and minister to the person, and it wasn't long before everyone was smiling and laughing and ready to go to battle together. I noticed that no one looked down on the person who needed ministry. In fact, ministering to them personally showed us how valuable and precious they were to the Lord, revealed the gifts they carried, and what an important part they played in our group. Times like these knitted our hearts together, increased our unity, and our prayers of agreement became more powerful.

I saw the benefit of personal ministry when it was needed, and it wasn't long before I was the person who needed personal ministry! There have been times when The Circle encouraged me to open up and get healed and delivered of something. Just like anyone else in the group who might be having a personal problem that was hindering their ability to agree in prayer, they did not want to pray about anything until I was set straight. They knew something was bothering me, holding me back, and therefore holding all of us back.

Now I was the head of this group, who were usually all women, and I was a man too. As a man and as a leader, it was very tempting to just pull rank and tell them they were wrong, that it wasn't important, or that it wasn't their business. But in my heart I knew they had hit upon something that needed attention in my life. I decided to swallow my pride and trust God, and I'm glad I did. Whether it was getting healed of an old wound or being released from a lie of the enemy, their ministry caused me to grow as a son of God, which made me a better leader and minister. I not only felt better and more confident to pray, but also it changed the atmosphere and strengthened the agreement of our prayers.

The other thing I noticed was that after I submitted to the prayers of The Circle, they didn't disrespect me or look down on me. I didn't have any problem maintaining my authority as their leader. It was the opposite. They honored me more because I had humbled myself before God and them to face a weakness or a problem and get free. In the end I was stronger and better, and so they found it easier to follow me.

Taking instruction, correction, or rebuke from those they lead is something many leaders will never do; and it is not God's way. The position we hold in the body of Christ doesn't mean we are better or worse than anyone else. We are all growing up in God. All of us need instruction, encouragement, correction, and a rebuke from time to time, and sometimes other leaders we look up to and admire may not be the ones God chooses to help us grow up (especially if we have pride issues).

If our eyes and ears are attuned to the Holy Spirit, we will recognize His helping hand in the person He sends to minister to us about a certain issue—and it might be someone who works for us or even someone who just got saved. It is hard enough to take instruction from an elder, but when someone who serves under our authority comes to us, that is really hard on the flesh!

All I can say is, from my experience you have to look to God and be humble toward Him and His other servants. You never know who will have the key to your problem, your deliverance, and your future.

PRAYER JOINS HEARTS TOGETHER

The Circle has become a foundational part of my life as well as my ministry. Through the years we have experienced just about every kind of victory and defeat you can experience as prayer warriors. There have been tears and mourning as we felt the pain and suffering of others we were interceding for. We have had to say good-bye to several precious and beloved warriors who went home to be with the Lord. There have been heated discussions and disagreements that had to be resolved. And there have been times of discouragement and frustration when we were trying to stay faithful to what God was calling us to do without always knowing what He was doing or whether or not our prayers were answered.

Mostly, though, what I cherish are the many powerful moments when we all knew clearly what God wanted us to do and our hearts were filled with the joy of doing it together. We declared and agreed with God's Word and sometimes immediately, sometimes in days or weeks or years, we saw the hand of God accomplish exactly what we prayed.

One time Jay and I went to an important meeting of leaders and emerging apostles from reservations all over North America. The Holy Spirit had shown Jay and me that the enemy was going to do everything in his power to upset people and cause strife and division, but members of The Circle were there to pray.

While Jay and I and the others were in the meeting, The Circle joined with prayer warriors from other ministries in another room. They all sought God together, and the Holy Spirit led them to pray and declare specific things. Later, when we talked about it, we discovered that everything they had prayed had been dealt with and discussed at our meetings. Because of their prayers, God's will was accomplished and the people in the conference got along fine.

The Circle has taught me many things—diligence, faithfulness, and the power of prayer—but mostly they have showed me that God moves through us powerfully when we are willing to humble ourselves before God and each other, when we are dedicated to living a life of honesty and integrity, and when we face our personal demons and overcome them. We do this in order to be the best we can be in our battle position, to take and fulfill our place in the body. Then together we can defeat the enemy and see God's will done on Earth as it is in Heaven.

CHAPTER 5

Always Go Forward, Never Look Back

"Always Go Forward, Never Look Back" is a song our Euchee people sang on the Trail of Tears. Many people don't realize that a lot of the Indians who were displaced during that terrible time were Christians, and this was a song of forgiveness and moving on to make a better future for our children. When it was sung, it released the mercy and grace of God over both those who blessed us and those who cursed us. Traditionally, the women would sing a verse, and then the men would sing a verse. Then they would sing together in unity. Together they released peace to the land they were walking over.

All the mature warriors I have known love this song. They understand this song. The idea of always going forward and never looking back was based on the Native belief of God's circle of life. He created our Earth and all the stars and planets in a round shape, in the shape of a circle. Even a baby in the womb is curled in a ball in the fetal position. The circle speaks of new life, ongoing life, and eventually returning to where we started. It shows how God's mercies are new every morning.

On the Trail of Tears our people never looked back and always looked forward in the knowledge and faith that one day God would bring them back to where they belonged. It might take generations, but that is the circle of life. They would be restored to the land He had called them to steward. As believers, my people knew that mankind started out pure, righteous, and holy. Then sin came in through Adam's disobedience, but we continued to walk forward in faith, knowing that one day God would return us to our original state. We would come full circle.

Finally Jesus came to die and pay the price for our sins, to show us the way back to the Father, back to the Garden, and back to our original state of purity, righteousness, and holiness. As believers, we have come back to the Father in our spirits, but our minds are being renewed with God's Word and are in the process of being transformed, and our bodies won't be fully restored until the resurrection. So we still have a journey to make. We still must go forward and not look back, having faith that one day we will come full circle and all will be as God originally intended when He created us.

THE POWER OF REPENTANCE

The people which sat in darkness saw great light; and to them which sat in the region and shadow of death light is sprung up.

From that time Jesus began to preach, and to say, Repent: for the kingdom of heaven is at hand.

Matthew 4:16-17

Jesus' first sermon was about repentance, so this is a big part of a warrior's life. I think of the word "repent" as meaning to turn back or go back to where you started, to that place that was pure and innocent, a place where you relied on God for everything and walked in His will. "Re" often means to repeat something or go back to the beginning, and "pent" reminds me of a penthouse, or a high place. When we repent, we return to the "high place" in God, where He created us to live.

The actual Greek word translated repent is *metanoeo*, which means to "change the mind...a true change of heart toward God."[1] When we repent, we change our minds and hearts. We change the way we think and feel about something. We change what we believe, and then we act according to what we now believe. We think on a higher, godly level; and when we think like God we will act like God.

Repenting is not feeling sorry you got caught, making excuses for what you did, or crying and wailing because you did wrong. You may be emotional when you repent, but repenting is not about emotions. It is recognizing and confessing you did wrong or you thought wrong and then restoring your life to the high life in God, coming back up to His level of living in the truth, doing what is right.

Jesus calls every human being to repentance because He is the one who leads us back to where we started, to that high place in God. We are born again when we receive Jesus as our

---

[1] See Spiros Zodhiates, *The Complete Word Study Dictionary: New Testament*, (Chattanooga, TN: AMG Publishers, 1992), #3340.

Savior and Lord, which means our spirits are made new and are filled with the Holy Spirit. From that point on, we begin to think more and more like God. We begin to develop the fruit of the Spirit, who is on the inside of us, and bring that fruit to the outside of us. Love, joy, peace, patience, gentleness, goodness, faith, meekness, and self-discipline begin to manifest in our life.

It sounds like I am contradicting myself when I say that we should always look forward and never look back, and yet I say that repentance means to go back. But repentance is making a course correction in where you are going. True spiritual warriors understand that repentance is realizing you have been moving in the wrong direction or you have been moving in the right direction with the wrong heart attitude. Repentance goes right along with always going forward and never looking back because it keeps you on God's path for your life and keeps your heart right.

There is nothing women warriors regard more highly than repentance! Repentance brings people to Jesus so that He becomes their Lord and Savior. Repentance can get people healed. Repentance can deliver people from bondage and sins of their past. So one of the things you will find in a woman warrior is a regular practice of repentance and the power and value of repentance.

All warriors recognize that repentance is part of living as a Christian because it is what makes you grow up and mature in God. The more you change your mind and heart to conform to God's mind and heart, the more you will become like Jesus. The more you are like Jesus, the more you glorify Him in all you do.

THE POWER OF FORGIVENESS

When a Native warrior was in their sacred place, seeking God and being cleansed and purified before a battle, they would take a feather attached to a leather string and hold it in the air. If the feather was still and did not move, they were not allowed to go to war; but if the wind blew the feather back and forth in a complete forward and backward motion, it was a sign the wind or breath of God was with them.

He lays the beams of His upper chambers in the waters;
He makes the clouds His chariot;
He walks upon the wings of the wind;
He makes the winds His messengers,
Flaming fire His ministers.

Psalm 104:3-4 NASB

The wind or breath of God, the power of the Holy Spirit, is with the woman warrior who walks in forgiveness, refuses to be offended, and rejects any temptation to become bitter. Because women are emotional, I have seen them struggle with their emotions when they are hurt, rejected, frustrated, offended, angry, jealous, envious, or feel betrayed. But true warriors know the power of forgiveness. They know how God forgave them and continues to forgive them, and so they draw on Him to forgive. They know that if they walk in forgiveness, they will be like that feather, free to move forward as God wants them to move in His power.

It is hard to pray right when you are mad at somebody or upset about something. Ecclesiastes 10:4 NASB says, "If the ruler's temper rises against you, do not abandon your position, because composure allays great offenses." When a person says or does something you don't like, the Bible tells you to remain calm, forgive, and hold your position. If you do that, your composure "allays great offenses." Forgiving keeps you from being offended and locks the enemy out of your life.

Women warriors know that when they don't forgive someone, they put themselves on the opposite side of God. He is forgiving and forgives us. When we are not forgiving, we are not like Him. We are not partaking of His divine nature. We are partaking of the devil's nature! The devil never forgives. He is the one who condemns us, constantly reminding us of our sins and faults and weaknesses. He will also try to get us to not forgive someone else, to condemn them and always remember all the terrible things they did to us.

There is nothing worse than a soldier who has a greater battle and more pain and torment on the inside than what's going on outside. They are so filled with bitterness that their strength is gone before they even draw their sword. That's why warriors aren't allowed to quarrel among themselves. They are required to forgive immediately, settle their differences quickly, and in that way maintain the unity of their military unit.

A woman warrior whose allegiance is truly to God and the authorities He has set in her life will always forgive. If there has been a misunderstanding, if she has been misinformed, if someone displeases her or even threatens her, she looks to the Lord for His wisdom. She waits upon Him and refuses to become offended.

Looking diligently lest any man fail of the grace of God; lest any root of bitterness springing up trouble you, and thereby many be defiled.

Hebrews 12:15

A root of bitterness springs up when we refuse to forgive, and it troubles us as well as everyone around us. When I'm praying with someone and I detect a note of bitterness, or if I hear bitterness in my words or feel bitterness in my heart as I'm praying, I stop and deal with that thing. Otherwise God will not hear my prayers.

If you refuse to forgive someone you have left your post. You have stopped fighting the good fight of faith. You are no longer moving forward because you are obsessed with the past. Did you know that walking in forgiveness is just as much spiritual warfare as taking authority over a demon on your land? In fact, if you don't walk in forgiveness, you better just stop praying and believing God for anything. Your prayers are not being heard. And you are letting everyone down, especially the Lord.

In order to move forward and do what God has called you to do, you cannot look back and keep anger or bitterness in your heart. Jesus told His disciples in Matthew 10:14 that if anyone rejected them and the message they brought, they should just kick the dust off their feet and move on—always move forward and never look back. You are to kick offenses out of your life the moment you realize they are there. Then you can walk in victory on the inside of you, and your prayers will be heard.

HONORING THE TIME

Women warriors understand the circle of life, always going forward, never looking back. They conceive and give birth. They nurse and nurture and teach their children. They watch them grow and become adults. And through all of this they experience labor pains, personal sacrifice, heartbreak, and the agony of separation when that child finally leaves home. They know what it means to fight for the souls of their children, to war with the enemy of their souls. And they know the joy of seeing their prayers answered.

Women warriors also know that if they are not in God's will, if their hearts are not right with Him and with His people, then their prayers will not be heard. If their prayers are not heard, they war in vain. Their efforts are for nothing. And other than evil, nothing makes a woman warrior angrier than wasted time and effort! They want every moment of their lives to count for the kingdom of God.

Women warriors are very conscious of time. They have a great respect for God's timing and honor that. In 2 Timothy

4:2 Paul tells us to be "instant in season" and "out of season." It is important for warriors to know the season they are in and be faithful to it. When in season, we don't wait. We take advantage of the opportunities that God has set before us. When out of season, when we don't see any opportunities, we don't slip away from our post. We stand our ground and wait for the Holy Spirit to lead us. We continue doing what we know to do and wait for further instructions.

To every thing there is a season, and a time to every purpose under the heaven:

A time to be born, and a time to die; a time to plant, and a time to pluck up that which is planted;

A time to kill, and a time to heal; a time to break down, and a time to build up;

A time to weep, and a time to laugh; a time to mourn, and a time to dance;

A time to cast away stones, and a time to gather stones together; a time to embrace, and a time to refrain from embracing;

A time to get, and a time to lose; a time to keep, and a time to cast away;

A time to rend, and a time to sew; a time to keep silence, and a time to speak;

A time to love, and a time to hate; a time of war, and a time of peace.

Ecclesiastes 3:1-10

The most powerful warriors understand that knowing God's time can make the difference between a great victory and a heartbreaking defeat. The passing of time causes their patience and trust in God to grow. The issue of time will cause them to either take their lives in their own hands or turn their lives over to God. And every true warrior knows they will never be safe in their own hands. They must be in God's hands to be protected, to have peace, and to be able to fight righteously. So they wait. They choose to be patient. They trust God to lead them at the right time.

When God's time is honored, a woman warrior can focus on the future in the right way. She can wait, knowing that standing her ground is still moving forward in God. Inside she is moving forward in patience and faith; and it is through patience and faith that she receives what God has given her (Hebrews 6:12).

DYING TO SELF

Women warriors know they cannot go into spiritual battle for anyone else if they haven't won the battle with their own flesh. If their flesh is alive in any way it will hinder them in warfare. They must reckon it dead. If their old, carnal self is influencing them, that means they are looking back. They are not moving forward. But if they are dead to themselves and completely alive to God, they are moving forward and there is nothing the enemy can do to hurt them because he can't kill a person who is already dead!

In the Old Testament prayer warriors would do all kinds of physical things that represented putting their flesh or their selfish nature to death. They would cry and wail, tear their clothes, wear sackcloth, sprinkle dust or ashes on themselves, shave their heads or pluck out the hair on their head or their beard, stop washing themselves, fast, or not wear any jewelry or ornaments. Some might even cut themselves or sit in silence for days.

Thank God, in the New Testament we don't need to do all these outward things to crucify our flesh, but sometimes dealing with our own hearts is harder! We know God looks on the heart, and circumcision is of the heart—that is where He needs to cut away the flesh. The Holy Spirit inside us deals with our hearts through the Word of God. It is the Word that cuts away the flesh.

All scripture is given by inspiration of God, and is profitable for doctrine, for reproof, for correction, for instruction in righteousness:

That the man of God may be perfect, thoroughly furnished unto all good works.

2 Timothy 3:16-17

Women warriors love God's Word for many reasons. They know it is the way to know God's will, so that is how they know how to pray about an issue. They know His Word carries His power and changes circumstances, situations, and environments. But most of all, they know His Word changes them. His Word gives them the ability to become dead to their old, carnal desires and to live fully by His Spirit. Then they can be powerful warriors.

FROM MOURNING TO DANCING

I have seen many warriors, men and women, go through many battles. Both men and women can get emotional and go through very hard times in intercession. But women have a special way of carrying someone else's burden, of feeling their pain and refusing to let go until they know God's Word is released into that life and the miracle is on its way.

They that sow in tears shall reap in joy.

He that goeth forth and weepeth, bearing precious seed, shall doubtless come again with rejoicing, bringing his sheaves with him.

Psalm 126:5-6

Tears and mourning don't necessarily move the heart of God. His Word spoken from a heart of faith is what moves Him. The Word is the precious seed women warriors plant in the Earth to change lives.

Tears and mourning are not for God's benefit; they are for ours. They release the compassion of God in us and draw us closer to each other. When a woman warrior begins to weep for the one we are praying for, all hearts are touched. The love and healing compassion of God begin to flow. It is a wonderful thing when this happens. It is a spiritual atmosphere where God can work freely because everyone has forgotten themselves and are only interested in seeing God's will done.

Because we are dead to ourselves, we can mourn and weep and intercede with pure hearts. We can hear the Holy Spirit more clearly and follow Him more closely. Our unity and agreement are established, and we know God is moving to perform His Word in that situation or in that person's life. Then comes the time when the warriors know the battle is won, and their mourning turns to dancing.

Thou hast turned for me my mourning into dancing: thou hast put off my sackcloth, and girded me with gladness;

To the end that my glory may sing praise to thee, and not be silent. O Lord my God, I will give thanks unto thee for ever.

Psalm 30:11-12

It is a sight to behold when a woman warrior or a bunch of women warriors know they have pressed through to defeat the enemy and win the victory! There can be tears of joy. There can be whooping and hollering. There can be dancing and singing praises to God. There can be shouts of "Praise the Lord! Thank You, Jesus! Hallelujah! Glory to God!" And sometimes there is just a quiet, peaceful moment when they smile that radiant smile of knowing God's will is done.

I have witnessed all these things in the women warriors I have known, and I feel sorry for the men who have missed out on the blessing of praying or ministering with a woman warrior. She understands the circle of life. She refuses to look back and presses on in what God has called her to do. And she inspires everyone around her to be all they were created to be in God.

Final Word:

A Woman Warrior's Legacy

There are many things women warriors leave behind when they go on to their great rewards in Heaven. They have left a trail of answered prayers that have changed the lives of everyone in their path, as well as prayers that will be answered long after they have left this Earth. They have left spiritual children and grandchildren and sometimes great-grandchildren, who are serving and loving God with all their hearts. They have left friends and neighbors whose lives were richer and better because of them. In some cases whole cities, nations, or the world were impacted by the river of life that came to them through these women warriors.

When my mother was passing from this life into Heaven, she called me to her bedside one last time. She said, "Son, I want to teach you the Euchee word for 'I love you.'"

I said, "Mom, I know how to say 'I love you' in our language."

"No," she said, "This is different. It is *ninzo de tai ute*."

I asked her what that meant, and she said, "You are like a river of life to me, and without you I cannot exist."

You are like a river of life to me, and without you I cannot exist.

This is the greatest love we can experience in life. *Ninzo de tai ute* is Jesus. He is a river of life to us, and without Him we cannot exist. We cannot live life to the fullest, now and for eternity.

Then God gives us the women warriors, like my mother, who are also rivers of life to us, coming right out of the heart of Jesus. Without them, our lives would be dry, lifeless, unfruitful, and without joy or fulfillment.

Only Jesus can tell us all the wonderful things the women warriors in our lives have done. It might have been just a short prayer, "God protect them," as they sent us off to school. It might have been a sigh in their hearts that said, "Lord, this is too much for me. Please take care of my friend. I release her to You. I trust You with her." It might have been a cry of "Jesus! Help him!" when they discerned their husbands were in trouble at work. It might have been that simple truth from God's Word they shared, which the Holy Spirit used to save someone. Or it might have been the sweet compassion of God's healing power flowing out of them as they prayed for someone who was sick.

Wherever they go, women warriors leave a mighty trail. It is a trail of tears on which they always go forward and never look back. It is a trail of joy on which they recount victory after victory and give God all the glory. He is so great and so big and majestic in their hearts, they just can't see anything but how wonderful He is, how powerful He is, and how everything they are and do is in His hands.

Great is the love of the woman warrior, and great is her inheritance.

ABOUT THE AUTHOR

Negiel Bigpond was born November 7, 1949. He is a full-blood Euchee/Yuchi Indian, and is a fourth-generation minister of the Gospel. His Euchee name is *Au wau day,* which means Sky Hunter, One Who Seeks Vision. He has been in ministry since 1975 as Morning Star Ministries and has been both evangelist and pastor. He has evangelized close to 200 Native American reservations and currently serves as Apostle of Morning Star Church of All Nations, as well as giving apostolic oversight to other churches on and off the reservations in America.

Always having a heart for those in prison, Dr. Bigpond maintains a prison ministry and is a certified drug and alcohol abuse counselor. He is an accomplished musician and singer, who has recorded several albums. He has also received an honorary doctorate from Jacksonville Theological Seminary.

Dr. Bigpond has traveled to Washington, D.C., to testify before a Senate Committee on Resolution 15, which is a joint resolution of apology to Native peoples for ill-conceived policies and broken treaties with Indian tribes by the U.S. government. He has received various keys to cities and proclamations from governors and mayors for his work in the eastern United States, and he and Dr. Swallow were named among "Charisma's Christian Newsmakers of 2006." He has also been on the boards of the following ministries and provides an apostolic covering for many ministers as a member of C. Peter Wagner's International Coalition of Apostles:

Native American Apostolic Council—Dr. Jay Swallow, Chairman

Native American Resource Network—Jean Steffenson, Chairwoman

Operation Starting Line—Chuck Colson, Chairman

Intercessors of America—Gary Bergel, Chairman

National Prayer Committee—David Butts, Chairman

Oklahoma Apostolic Prayer Network—Dr. John Benefiel, Chairman

Dr. Bigpond has traveled worldwide, representing Christian Native Americans and preaching and teaching God's Word. Inspired through his involvement in Oklahoma Apostolic Prayer Network, he and Dr. Jay Swallow founded the Native America Circle of Prayer, now called the Native America Apostolic Prayer Circle, which establishes prayer teams who are skilled in spiritual warfare and intercession for the Native people and issues that concern them. He also established Spirit Wind, an annual day of prayer for the Five Civilized Tribes and their leaders. Today many more tribes gather for this event all across America.

God has also given Dr. Bigpond the vision of Two Rivers Native American Training Center, in which he is the president and co-founder with Dr. Swallow. The training center is a Christian training camp, raising up believers to war in the Spirit and defeat the enemy in their own lives, in the lives of others, in the affairs of cities and nations, and especially on the Indian reservations.

Dr. Bigpond and his wife Jan have three children, one daughter-in-law, two sons-in-law, and six grandchildren. They reside in the great metropolis of Hectorville, Oklahoma, on the land where Morning Star Church of All Nations and Two Rivers Native American Training Center also stand.

To contact Dr. Bigpond you may write:

P. O. Box 97

Bixby, OK 74008

call:

918-366-6735

e-mail:

tworivers@olp.net

New –
A great study for women's groups!

Now *Women Warriors* has a companion *Workbook!*

"This *Workbook* follows *Women Warriors* closely and can be a blessing to both the individual and a group.

"I suggest that each woman warrior consider this *Workbook* her private journal. The experience will be even more powerful if you participate in a group study and discuss each issue with other women warriors."

Negiel Bigpond

A great gift book that's full of information — and fun to read!

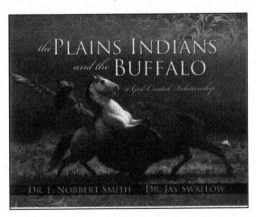

History. Biology. Photographic Record. Art. Ancient Stories.

This colorful book gives you an understanding
of all the factors
and diabolical schemes that led to the near extinction
of both the Indian culture and the buffalo.

And yet, they have overcome every challenge.

Read about this amazing restoration!

PERFECT CIRCLE PUBLISHING
MISSION STATEMENT

The mission of Perfect Circle Publishing is to give voice to Native American believers in Jesus Christ. It is our conviction by the Holy Spirit that when the First Nations take their place in the body of Christ, and as their gifts and callings come forth, revival will come to America. Then the church in America—men, women, and children of all cultures and colors—will arise as a glorious light to all nations of the Earth, proclaiming and celebrating the Gospel of Jesus Christ as our Creator originally intended.

To order more books, please visit our website:
www.perfectcirclepublishing.com